COLLEC

POETRY

*For my stalwart and indefatigable friend Tim.
You are a truly unique individual, keep on being
you and doing that unique thing that you do.*

*Thank you for unreservedly buying this copy
entirely on spec. I hope everything is well
with you and wish you nothing but the
best in the future!*

*Don't forget to let me know when you
spot the typographical errors!!!*

*With love and affection
always...*

*Shaun O'Neill
and
Fiona
xx
x*

xxx

Chiado Publishing

chiadopublishing.com

Nov. 2013

All characters and events in this publication, other than those clearly in the public domain, are ficticious and any resemblance to real persons, living or dead, is purely coincidential.

chiadopublishing.com

U.K | U.S.A | Ireland
Kemp House
152 City Road
London
EC1CV 2NX

Spain
Centro de Negocios Edificio España
Plaza de España, Nº 5 - 6
37004 Salamanca
España

France | Belgium | Luxembourg
Porte de Paris
50 Avenue du President Wilson
Bâtiment 112
La Plaine St Denis 93214
France

Germany
Kurfürstendamm 21
10719 Berlin
Deutschland

Portugal | Brazil | Angola | Cape Verde
Avenida da Liberdade
Nº 166, 1º Andar
1250-166 Lisboa
Portugal

Web: www.chiadopublishing.com | www.chiadoglobal.com

Title: Entropy and Me
Author: Shaun O'Neill

Graphic Design Ps_design – Departamento Gráfico

Printed and Bound by: *Chiado Print*

ISBN: 978-989-51-0617-2
Legal Deposit n.º 362650/13

SHAUN O'NEILL

ENTROPY AND ME

Chiado Publishing

For Mum, wherever you may be.

CONTENTS

ENTROPY AND ME

I've got fourteen guitars and piles of old books.
My boiler won't boil and my cooker won't cook.
I've got a lovely big telly, that I never watch.
There's a drawer in my kitchen stuffed full of odd socks.

I've got a mini-disc player that's gone out of fashion.
And I think my libido has ran out of passion.
There's a spoon for a door-handle since the other one broke.
I've got loads of bad habits and tell really crap jokes.

I hate doing dishes and washing my clothes.
In Winter I collect lots of crows from my nose.
No food in my freezer but its chock-full of ice.
I eat ready-made meals that don't taste very nice.

My clocks have stopped working so I can't tell the time.
The back of the fridge is encrusted with grime.
My neighbours are fearful as I make lots of noise.
And I can't get a job so I'm still unemployed.

My washing machine has just gave up the ghost.
But I can't say I'm bothered 'cos I hate that the most.
I look at the stars with my big telescope.
And I'm really amazed at how well I still cope.

I've had a can of baked beans in the cupboard for years.
It gets on my tits that Mach 3's are so dear.
I don't own a bed, go to sleep in a bag.
And I'm not very nice when I lose my rag.

I eat when I'm hungry, I sleep when I'm tired.
When I read a book, it leaves me inspired.
I don't go to church, so I don't talk to God.
And most of the people I know think I'm odd.

I've got lots of note-books that I fill up with shite.
I'm never much pleased with the stuff that I write.
I try to pen poems that mostly don't rhyme.
It gives me a pleasure that is hard to define.

I hoard loads of old crap I can't bear to throw out.
My ceiling needs paint and my bathroom needs grout.
I've lost all the plugs so I can't fill the sink.
And that's why I hate doing dishes I think.

My back-yard's untended, a haven for weeds.
My dust-bin needs mending, and it's missing a wheel.
I can see up the entry since the panel blew down.
And I'm sure that my brick-work is becoming unsound.

I've got a car on the front that I don't like to drive.
Because motoring costs are excessively high.
My smoke alarm beeps 'cos the battery is flat.
So one day I'll burn, and that will be that.

When I have a bath, my pipes makes a noise.
My angle-poise lamp has lost all its poise.
I admit that the house could do with a dust.
And the bike in my shed has now started to rust.

I'm fifty years old which is cause for alarm.
I feel a bit grumpy and I've lost all my charm.
My patience is thinning but I've still got my hair.
But my eye-sight is going and my hearing's impaired.

I like Kentucky Fried Chicken, I get the munchies a lot.
But I don't like Mc Donalds and I smoke too much pot.
I talk to myself when there's no one else there.
So I'm seeing a shrink but I get on her nerves.

When I wake in the mornings, I burp and I fart.
So I go for a shite and then watch it depart.
Then I have twenty brews and some bacon on toast.
And think how nice it would be to live life as a ghost.

DECEPTION

As mistletoe's alluring bloom.
The Roses thorn beneath the green.
The beautiful anemone,
The deadly sting concealed within.

The Sirens call, the mermaids air.
To doom do they entice them there.
In guile they lead into despair.
Their souls entrapped and minds ensnared.

The widow spider seeks her mate.
To death, she lures him to his fate.
With her fangs she consummates.
In marriage she is profligate.

The cuckoo searching for a nest.
Instinctively she finds the best.
Her murderous offspring is her bequest.
The downy warmth does she infest.

The orchid exudes a sweet perfume.
Bright petals flower in pulchritude.
And motionless within that bloom.
The mantis waits in verisimilitude.

The folly of true lusts desire.
The temptation of the carnal loin.
In faith and trust are indisposed.
And in the end at once defiled.

In truth these beauties rare and true.
As parasites with no virtue.
The lethal venom they infuse.
With bitterness they do imbue.

Beware the deadly nightshade then.
The suns warm halo I befriend.
The pure light incorruptible.
As integrity I do defend.

FACEBOOK

I need a fix of Face-Book, to help me through the day.
I've got a million opinions, but nothing much to say.
I've got a thousand unknown friends, and some of them are
[gay.
God I need a fix of Face-Book, to get me through today.

I took a picture of my dinner, all lovingly prepared.
With a list of the ingredients, incongruously shared.
When it's passed through my digestive tract, and my bowels
[they had stirred.
I'd be sure that I record the fact, and take a picture of the turd.

My profile lists my hobbies, wide ranging and diverse.
Squeaky clean and interesting, there's nothing there perverse.
My faults are few, no frailty to mar my argent shine.
My 2D world for all to see, I put it all on-line.

I'm immersed in unreality, my virtual farm I must attend.
Race jelly beans that bounce through streams,
Then compete them with my "friends".
My hashish farm is doing well, I wish that it were real.
If I could trade on line I'd do just fine, get myself a better deal.

These hallowed pages beckon for the swift stroke of my
[keys.
My benevolence and kindness are there for all to see.
A lovely world for all to share, and no one disagrees.
No banality or frivolity or mediocrity.

Now and then I get the urge.
To rave and rant and scream and splurge.
Controversially I spout and shout, I don't know what life's
[about.
Now some of you may get irate, with the rows that I initiate,
As your friendship I deactivate, then two days later reinstate.

Electronic curtain twitching, a new phenomenon.
I can gossip with alacrity at all the "goings on".
I can leave my cryptic messages to let you ponder on.
Then stab you in the back my friend, the minute that your
[gone.

There's no need for me to log off, even when I'm not at home.
I post sad facts that don't detract, I can do it from my phone.
If Jesus uses Face-Book (I'm sure I've got Him as a mate).
J.H.Christ@fuckoff.com... it makes one contemplate.

I need a fix of Face-Book, I need it more than ever.
I can cover my ineptitude and make myself look clever.
And if I feel inferior or intellectually lame,
I'll just slag someone with fewer "friends" and play my
[farming game.
Oh Face-Book loyal, Face-Book true, I put all my life
[on-line for you.
The last time that I interact..if ever I may fall from grace...
My Face-Book funeral will be ace!

THE MOON

The Moon is dead and sterile,
A hostile, airless place.
This desolate environment,
Spinning 'round us out in space.

A billion eyes look up,
To see that old familiar face.
From each new generation,
Of the lonely Human Race.

Its seas contain no water,
Its skies as black as ink.
Its landscape holds no colour,
Its volcanoes all extinct.

On the day-side, in its heavens,
The Earth hangs in the sky.
Ever constant in position,
Its phases changing by the by.

It has observed our evolution,
With its cold impassive eyes.
For a hundred thousand years,
It has travelled through our skies.

And four billion years ago,
It did watch this Earth evolve.
Its orbit slowly matching,
To the rate that it revolves.

Such a very strange coincidence,
It is the same size as the sun.
The lesser light that rules the night,
When the day on Earth is done.

As it circles through the night sky,
As now we can predict.
At such times can orbits cross,
To produce a rare eclipse.

In stark contrast to our home,
This Earth, the jewel in the crown.
In our crowded atmosphere,
Upon the Moon exists no sound.

Now derelict and battered,
History written on its face.
The violence it has suffered,
Etched forever in that place.

As it drags around the oceans,
So our seas still fall and rise.
To this slow and steady rhythm,
Life on Earth has synchronised.

To men the Moon has beckoned,
With many hypnotised.
The possibility of going there,
So often fantasised.

Now there are foot-prints on the Moon,
Pressed into that ancient soil.
Imprinted there forever,
No winds there to despoil.

Men have walked upon its surface,
And safely have returned.
And all are in agreement,
Of the one thing we have learned.

That the Earth is small and fragile,
The only place we can call home.
This tiny little planet,
Made of fire and air and stone.

Revolving around a star,
In this silent vast expanse.
The only world we know,
Where life has got a chance.

FUNERAL

Bright sunshine glints from the roof of the hearse
As it rounds the corner into the crematorium.
Behind it, a cortège of brightly coloured cars snake single
[file.

There is no comfort in black.
Colour is life.

All around, people pass by.
Vapour trails evaporate in the intense blue sky.
Buses, shops, bustle...
Life goes on...

Birdsong drifts into the the open car window
As humanity clatters relentlessly onward...
A stark contrast that enlivens the senses
And gives momentary relief...

As the entourage files in, the previous one files out,
One less in their number.
And behind them,
In their rear-view mirrors,
A puff of wistful smoke rises heavenward
From the crematorium chimney...

All in black,
Neatly turned out,
They gather in the warm afternoon sun
To talk quietly amongst themselves.
Sons, daughters, sisters, brothers, aunts, uncles,
Fathers, Mothers... they come...

Inside...

Stained glass refracts the summer light
Into a carpet of shimmering rainbows on the plush-piled floor
And the space within is filled to the brim
With almost tangible thought...

A coffin.
A priest.
And a neatly folded-back velvet curtain
Are all that remain between the Heavens and the Earth.
And the corpse in the coffin, out of which I came,
Lies,
Indifferent,
Facing the azure flawless sky.

The black congregation mourn the vacated shell
And join in the lurid worship of a non-existent god.

They pray, as the priest prattles away
The words sink like stones
Drowned in multi-coloured crepuscular rays
Streaming in through the stained-glass windows
From the real world outside.
A young woman with a baby is sat in front of me.
The baby over her shoulder gurgles and smiles
Inside, I laugh at the irony of it all.

In the front pew
My immediate "family"
Tearful and red-eyed,
Affix the image of my mothers coffin
Indelibly into their minds.
I look into the baby's gleaming, sun glinted eyes
Innocent and wide
And am comforted.

They recite the lords prayer and the 23rd psalm
And ask for forgiveness, as we whirl through the void.
In the infants eyes I see infinity
A billion possibilities
That will one day turn to ash and light
As we all must do.

What do we do on this Earth?
We bicker, and gossip
Grumble, gripe.
Complain in the strongest possible terms
About how shit life is.
We dream of winning the lottery
Of buying expensive things we can't afford
Borrow money for holidays abroad.
Everything you need is here
In the eyes of this baby smiling at me.

My Uncle John rises to say a few words
But he must be brief, as god is pushed for time today.
Next to the coffin
He stands and talks.
Not of the corpse within
But of the life that was.
He celebrates the life of my Mum

And for a moment, I am proud.
Memories of childhood swim before my eyes
Rare, happy moments materialise
And the baby giggles, as if she can see them too.
Then, he closes his speech and in the silence that ensues,
he begins to clap.
The joyful noise breaks the sullen silence
And all at once, that sacred space is filled to the roof with
the sound of
Applause.
And my Mum takes one last encore before the velvet curtain
closes for the final time.
After the service, they talk amongst themselves once more
My brother and sisters tearful to the end.
Just an outside observer, a straggler am I.
Solitary as an oyster
Empty as the sky.

As the brightly coloured cars crawl out single file
The crematorium conveyor belt completes another lap.
As I cross the thresh-hold, a hearse is pulling in
A multi-coloured snake with its iridescent skin
And I look through my rear view mirror
To catch that wistful veil of smoke...

ATOMS

If we are made of atoms, electrons, protons, neutrons...
Which in turn are made from smaller things called quarks
[with charms so strange.
And they all fit together so that our minds and bodies
[contemplate...
Then how, and why are atoms, so conveniently arranged?

And these tiny specks of matter, fused together inside stars.
Then flung into the universe, a billion years ago...
Obeying laws of gravitation, attracting through the void.
I do not see how they made me, how do the atoms know?

Since space is mostly emptiness, and atoms mainly empty
[space.
Electromagnetically joined to share expanding space and
[time.
So the atoms of my body, my hands and heart and face...
Have been around for aeons, and were never really mine!

These atoms can be counted, and they number ninety two.
From the lightest to the densest, they constructed me and you.
They didn't get instruction, they knew not what to do.
Yet here I sit and ponder on just how the fuck they knew!

DNA is made of atoms, this amazing twisty stuff!
It arranges other atoms into things that live and breathe!
Could it be that God's a particle of consciousness and light?
And exists for all eternity, in everything we see?

Are atoms made of consciousness, does God dwell within
[us all?
Is the fibre of your being as old as time itself?
Vibrating strings of energy, unto entropic death.

GOLDEN SLUMBER

I want to stare.
Vacantly into space.
Deny every thought.
Empty my head and take a rest from myself.
Switch off, you TWAT.

I want to be a CHAV.
Think CHAV thoughts.
No notional prioritisation.
Limited communication.
Stupid and happy.
Dumb and daffy.
What bliss there must be in ignorance.

To mong*... perchance, to catch flies.
What pulchritude there is in stupidity.
I envy the innocence of idiots.
The happiness of half-wits.
The monotony of morons.
The idyll of the imbecile.

---

*Local expression for staring vacantly into space.

The whole of the world.
Contained for them within a two metre diameter, opaque
[indestructible bubble.
To sleep the sleep of the innocent.
That Golden Slumber.
Of the truly stupid.

INSURED

What a racket, what a scam.
Subscribe to this Insurance plan.
We'll make a packet, hand on hand.
With language you can't understand!

Insure yourself, your car, your cat,
Your life, your house, your health.
Your television, mobile phone,
The Insurance company's wealth.

Insure your kids, your holidays,
Your mortgage payments too.
Take out a plan without delay,
Or grief may come to you.

Protect the items that you buy,
You're covered for another year.
Ignore the twelve month guarantee,
Put our profits in the clear.

If you can't afford the premiums,
Charge it monthly, as a loan.
With interest charges added on,
At interest rates unknown.

Insure your teeth, your cock and balls,
The bum-fluff up your arse.
Then you can smile with confidence,
Next time you light a fart.

Insure your drains, they may well block,
And fill your house with pooh.
Your boiler might blow up next week,
Make sure it's covered too.

Our plans are comprehensive,
As long as you don't claim.
If you do, your policy,
Will double all the same.

Can I insure my sense of humour?
It's getting well beyond a joke.
Can I take out some insurance,
To protect me when I'm broke?

Cars have to be insured,
It is legally required.
Now you can charge me double,
Next year when its expired.

What a con, a trick, a perfect ruse!
It's money for "old rope"!
From a million paying "customers",
What a load of dopes!

Now I'm fully covered, head to toe,
As long as I stay in the house.
I can ill afford the payments,
On the cover to go out!

It is true that there is blood in stones?
Insurance companies bleed them dry!
That's why we're here, so make a claim,
In the event that you may die.

DO IT!

Work... don't make me laugh!
A job?
An opinion?
A gob?
A bedroom, a guitar, an allowance, a bar?
Another bedroom player?
A philosopher with Face-Book degree.
Oh Mummy look!
Look at me!

Work... don't make me laugh!
Hard physical graft... hardy har har!
Thirty years for murder?
I should have killed you all.
But no...
I towed the line... got my head down.
I did... the biz.

Talk... cheap and disposable.
Is there anything worth remembering?
Is anything worth the cost?
So I worked.
And I lost.

Bedroom... computer... high-speed connection.
Thanks Mummy, I love you Daddy!
That particular bubble of mine never existed...
So don't expect a POP.
Fuck off... away from me...
And wait for the pop.

Ice... snow and rain... it's 6 am again.
And the world is full of cunts.
Cunts... applying lipstick at 80 m.p.h.
Cunts... watching other cunts in traffic jams.
Cunts... taking the piss out of other cunts.
Cunts... calling each other cunts.

Work... don't make me laugh!
Barrack-room lawyers.
Armchair critics.
Bedroom philosophy.
Back-seat drivers.
Face Book sociology.
Fuckin' stay-at-home do-gooders.
Tweeting Twittering Twats.
Me.Me.Me.Me.

Social networking?
A lot of ego's jostling for pole-position.

Work?
A lot of ego's back-stabbing each-other for pole-position.

Philosophy?
A few ego's trying to make most of the other ego's look stupid.

Music?
A lot of ego's playing guitars wanting to be stars.

Talk?
A lot of ego's blabbing away and only listening to themselves.

Jealousy?
All the ego's that didn't get to the starting line.

So...
Don't say anything.
Do your stuff.
Do it as much as you can.
WHATEVER your stuff is... do it.
DO IT NOW.

THE BOMB

What a piece of work, this mind of man!
It calculates and forward-plans.
It comprehends and understands.
Co-ordinates with eye and hand.
It fathoms in its dark recess, it never sleeps, it never rests.
Curiosity, it quests.
The enquiring mind of man!

This paradox of human kind, its spirit blighted yet divine!
The mind and soul at once combined.
This seer of the future... blind!
It sees into infinity, it ponders its divinity.
It wallows in its vanity!
This paradox of man.
This paragon of evolution.
This scientific revolution.
Applying lightning-fast solutions to the problems of
[mankind.
It thought of manual labour less.
Designed machines to do the rest.
With profit it became impressed.
The imperfect mind of man.

Its mind now so inquisitive.
It saw how things were relative.
It pondered this imperative and converted it to light!
The power of the atom fused, could liberate the world, if
[used.
Yet corrupted power is soon abused.
The shallowness of men.

Invisible power for all the world.
A fruitful bounty to be shared.
The energy of MC squared, the ingenuity of men!
The problems of the world so solved.
The steadfast hearts of men resolved.
His virtuous nature so extolled!
The generosity of man!.

Revelation made them paranoid.
They built bombs and were over-joyed.
Before too long they were deployed by the arrogance of man.
The peaceful city was destroyed and sixty thousand
[humanoids.
Were turned to ashen silhouettes...

In a second vaporised and the Western world was mesmerised.
In an instant sixty thousand lives.
Were snuffed out of existence.
And the power that this signified to the corruptible and
[hypnotised.
All at once was recognised.
The worthlessness of men.
Their scheming minds connived and planned.
The weak gave in to their demands.
And in this way the greed expands.
The iniquity of man.

War begins with Ice-cold threats.
Cold and hard, their secrets kept.
And the poorest of the wretches wept.
And the wedge was driven home.

And backs were stabbed and agents crept.
Propaganda used to great effect.
And in ignorance, the people slept.
And thought not of their fates.

The planet's wired to detonate.
The scientists coolly calculate.
How long the world will radiate.
After all the bombs have dropped.
And when the fall-out propagates.
For millennia to contaminate.
It may already be to late.
For the madness to be stopped.

WANKER

There once was a fella called Hank.
He liked to indulge in a wank.
He would do it for hours, his masturbatory powers,
Were astounding to be perfectly frank.

He would wank in the wardrobe at home.
When he knew that he would be alone.
As he come in his pants, he would jiggle and dance,
As he thought of his cock being blown.

He was a tosser of par excellence.
As he took up his usual stance.
He could shoot all his sperm, with his John Thomas firm,
And his knee-caps would tremble and dance.

He would toss-off first thing in the morning.
Then he noticed his nob was deforming.
It bent to the right, 'cos he pulled it all night.
But his stiffy was always reforming.

His balls were the size of two onions.
Soon his underpants couldn't contain 'em.
His scrotum was huge, and so it caused a deluge.
And his cock was developing bunions.

He was proud of his big purple glans.
As he lovingly took it to hand.
After he masturbated, it was never deflated.
He could make it stand proud on demand.

What became of this fella called Hank?
In middle-age his prick became very lank.
It wouldn't go rigid and his life became frigid.
Now he can't even fire out blanks.

And the moral of this tale is true.
It could happen to me or to you.
If you wank night and day,you might wear it away.
And its sure to fall off if you do.

TECHNOPHILLIAC

I love technical specification.
I don't want simplification.
I want my **MIDI** implementation.
Included in my documentation.

Give me heavy technical reading.
How are those fast reactors breeding?
Don't forget those tolerance readings.
I must read those, don't touch that dial!
I see your buffer's over-flowing.
Your data transfer rates are slowing.
That hard-disc light, it keeps a glowing.
You've got a few corrupted files!

My oscillator's oscillating.
The wave-form is scintillating.
The diagnostic software's stating.
This machine's not up to spec!
Upgrade the main processor.
From mere student, to professor!
And don't forget the noise suppressor.
It only takes a micro-sec.

Analogue is prehistoric.
Digital is meteoric.
It makes me feel euphoric!
Those little queues of off's and ons.
As the bits and bytes get longer.
Microsoft make **LOTS** of wonga.
But is the operating system stronger?
Did we all fall for this con?

It doesn't seem to run much faster.
And you're flirting with disaster.
If you ever try to master.
Multi-tasking at one stroke.
All the tweaks and tricks are hidden.
Of the **C:>** prompt we've been ridden.
Access to "**DOS**" is now forbidden.
For an ordinary bloke.

I like musical equipment.
Eagerly, I wait my shipment.
Gladly I give full commitment.
To my favourite measurements.

Noise to signal ratio's.
Charts indicate the signal flow.
Schematic diagrams that show.
The output voltage paths.
A parametric equaliser.
The plug-in externaliser.
The sequencer with humaniser.
Number crunching, light-speed maths!

Compression types so large in number.
Reverbs, delays and pitch-shift wonders!
Tonight for me there'll be no slumber!
Pure technical ecstasy!
Can I tweak with your parameters?
The high-street stuff's for amateurs.
How I long to wind your armatures.
With perfect accuracy.

Decibels and Watts are ringing.
The speakers they are singing.
Oh the joy that this is bringing.
All in high fidelity!
All the circuit boards are thrumming.
Higher frequencies forthcoming.
The central processor is running,
Its instructions perfectly!

Behind all the quantum magic.
To me it still seems quite fantastic.
Its computing power frantic.
And it runs consistently!
To absorb this information.
Fills me with elation.
I revel in complication.
And the technicality!

HANG ON

I can't sleep.
It's like "A Nightmare On Elm Street."
When I close my eyes I go somewhere else.
I blink, and open my eyes to hyper-reality.
A different, yet familiar place.

I dream of people hanging in formation.
They sing sweet music and dance in the air.
The purest music they weave.
Moving together, they make kaleidoscopic ballet.
As they hang suspended in the ether.
Like angels.

I blink again and am trapped.
Betwixt fire and death.
I am in the World Trade Centre.
One of those poor people on the upper floors.
To burn, or fly?
Flames to my right, blue sky to my left.
Gravity in-between.

It is a tenuous thread from which I hang.
And all around, the Blackness.
The total infathomability of it.
The absence of light, and hope.
And the choice that is no choice at all.
Hang on...
Or cut the thread.

THE FLY

Consider the Fly.
See his shiny, beady little eye.
His black chitinous frame and plastic-looking wings.
His purpose, his being, his ultimate fate?
Observe the Fly.

So tiny is he, and yet, he sees, he perceives,
As around the room he weaves,
His macroscopic brain, impelling him along.

What image through those faceted eyes?
What brain to comprehend them?

Behold his random movement,
Does he know, that he's a Fly?
He has blood and guts and nerve,
And he abides with me upon this world.
What kind of thought process goes on,
In the "mind" of this tiny, black speck?

Does he hunger, taste and touch,
Does such information pass as thought,
Through the swollen cortex in his head?
His meanderings important to him alone?
Or is he guided by instinct, a tiny machine?

Observe the Fly.
Try to be him.
To see where he goes, to see where he's been.
How does his hunger feel at that scale?
For his self preservation is it fear that prevails?
And does he have choices, and free will?

Is he aware of himself, or a tiny machine,
Programmed and wound up by his own DNA?
He has life and direction, takes up physical space,
Interacts with the world, he has earned his own place.

He takes to the air and alights on my leg,
Does he know I'm alive or aware of my form?
As I roll up a paper and climb into his head,
Can he understand that he soon will be dead?

There's a stain on my leg, tinged in dark red.
From my rolled-up newspaper, I can see tiny legs.
They do the Dance Of The Dying Fly.
Do you have the time, to reconsider The Fly?

TELLY

What's on telly?
(Shite... mostly every night)
Instant delight?
Entertainment... light?
Stars... (bright)
Celebrities... (trite)
Big brother... (fights)
And all things nice!

What's on tonight?

Horror films
(fright)
Documentaries
(insight?)
Big Brother... in spite?
Reality (shows) in real-time (piped)
Into your big BIG telly.

What's on in the morning? What's on?

Violence (graphic)
Porno (graphic)
National Geo(graphic)
Serials

Cereals, adverts (immaterial)
Angry chefs, The News
(depressed), old TV shows
(reprocessed), Jeremy Kyle
(confessed)... not impressed.
Ads (sad), soaps
(mad), lotteries
(bad), W.A.G's
(slags), M.P's
(blags), diets
(fads), we've all been had.

Horror (glamorised)
Scandal (sanitised)
Vandals (idolised)
Religion (sanctified)
Common sense? (pulverised)
Politics (polarised)
Film stars (beatified)
Homicide (sensationalised)
People (compartmentalised)
Homosexuals (sodomised)
Integrity (compromised)
Paternity (Bastardised)
Morality (crucified)

What's on telly?

The Brain (washing machine)
The end of thought... (abort)
Abort.

THE DARK ONES

In dark, dank places... they creep.
In black, blank places... they seep.
In corpulent greed... they thrive.
In virulence... they survive.

On ice-cold stares... they feed.
On benevolence... they breed.
Their hapless hosts... they mislead.
The gentle of spirit... they bleed.

The aimless souls... they descry.
Their shameless goals... they try.
Their painless holds... they apply.
The unfortunates... they die.

On suffering... they advance.
Then upon their graves... they dance.
They hide within the dark expanse.
Taking pride in greed and decadence.

Their poison eyes... they hide.
Their yellow lies... divide.
The hollow smiles... they snide.
Their hungry mouths... set wide.

Upon misfortune... .they grow fat.
They feast on it... like rats.

WHEN THE OIL HAS GONE

No more reciprocating pistons, going up and down.
No more precisely timed explosions, to turn the crankshaft
                                                    [round.
No more inductions or compressions.
No more ignitions or exhausts.
No more CO_2 emissions from this dwindling resource.

No traffic jams or accidents, or carnage on the roads.
No more road-rage, no more rushing.
No radiators to explode.
No more maintenance or servicing.
No MOT's to worry about.
No more petrol for our motorcars,
When the oil runs out.

No parking or inspectors.
No more tickets, fines or clamps.
No more speed-traps or detectors.
No more motor racing champs.
No McDonalds you can drive through.
No more delays caused by red lights.
No GPS to guide you, through ever darker nights.

No more global economics operated by the few.
No refineries or pipe-lines, to prepare the oil for use.
No more ozone, no more ice-caps, at either of the poles.
No more cities at sea-level, as rising waters take their tolls.

The greed of men is boundless.
They accumulate vast wealth.
No principles of business.
Obscene profits made in stealth.
As the oil supplies diminish.
And the petrol pumps dry up.
With every dollar squeezed.
Out of every single drop.

No more fly-wheels turning.
No more changing gear.
No four-stroke engines burning,
Or polluting year on year.
But all ready it's too late now.
The damage has been done.
The beginning of the ending,
Already has begun.

IGNITION

It's in the early hours, (as the seasons march), on their
[ceaseless turns...
As the sun spirals into Autumn and the Earth rotates once
[more into another dawn...
I stifle another yawn.

In the early morning, as neighbours sleep and dream, just
[before their waking moments...
Warm and snug in their beds, their memories hanging in
[threads...
Just moments away, from their rude awakenings.

In this twilight zone, a hundred thousand nascent alarm
[clocks tick...
Measuring moments in perfect quartz driven accuracy, this
[precise dawn chorus...
Waiting, to herald another day.

Outside, empty streets, full of empty cars... silence.
Whilst in the huddled houses they sleep, dreaming perhaps
[of better lives with better cars...
Before their rude awakenings.

As they approach the terminator, dark divider of night and
[day...
The coming wave of electronic shocks, pre-loaded into their
[alarm clocks...
Pistols ready to start the race again... and again.

In blissful slumber, oblivious...
Sleeping in voltage controlled tedium...
Snoring, farting, coughing and waiting to do someone else's
[bidding...

Consuming as they sleep, they dream of better things...
A hundred million key-rings lie on bed-side tables...
Waiting for ignition.

MOTHER

The womb I was formed in is dying,
In a sterile and colourless room.
In the waiting-room people are crying.
They say it will be over soon.

I wish they had made a connection,
When they cut my umbilical cord,
But all that I felt was rejection,
From the feelings you couldn't afford.

I find it hard to express my emotions,
From my moment of birth, to this day.
Through childhood denied this devotion,
I can't think of the right words to say.

Now the body that I was conceived in,
(The seed of the bad fruit unknown),
With the help of machines is still breathing,
But will depart from this world soon, alone.

Early memories smeared out and blurred,
"Family", just an alien word.
Other kids with their sisters and brothers,
Doing "things" with their Fathers and Mothers.

Nowhere could anyone touch me,
I constructed a world of my own.
I invented a framework around me,
And into this structure I've grown.

I fortified my complex defences,
From the earliest days I recall.
I'd interact with these alien people,
Through small holes in my internal wall.

The strongest of my recollections,
And this, would I never condone.
A calculated and thought-out detachment,
And this feeling of being alone.

In some ways, in my cold isolation,
I perfected my own ways to think.
So I justified my extrication,
With a nod or a smile or a blink.

My best mates were the walls of my bedroom,
I would read or invent and pretend.
And it shames me that I can't remember,
That my Mother was ever my friend.

No monochrome photograph memories.
No scrapbooks containing my face.
No identity handed down to me.
All evidence of me since erased.

I tried to be the best son I could be,
My paternity, I gave it no thought.
I deliberately locked it away,
Were it festered and grew into warts.

In your head, as your body is dying,
Is an image I'm yearning to see.
The face of my Father is fading.
Does his face now remind you of me?

I wish that I could be there with you,
Though you're now just a few miles from me.
To cross the vast distance between us,
Would take an infinity.

I am thinking of you, and am with you,
Even though we are so far apart.
Because in the end, you're my mother,
And will ever live on in my heart.

Alone we come into this world,
And draw comfort, from family and friends.
If things could be somehow so different,
I would be with you now at the end.

You are Mum, you are Dad,
All that I ever had.
You made me, I am here,
Have I turned out so bad?

Still deep in my heart, is a vacuum,
Impossibly hard to express.
This infinity that I have carried,
That I know can never egress.

Maybe somewhere in Time, I will see you,
And we could sit down and talk about things.
And the emptiness in my existence,
Be replaced with the light you may bring.

I have wished that we could be a family.
All these years of being estranged,
Have hardened my outer defences,
And left lots of things unexplained.

The womb that I grew in lies dying,
And there's nothing at all I can do.
If a thought could traverse through a light-year,
Then I send all these thoughts out to you.

For Mum, from her son... Shaun.

ONE SMALL STEP

(Neil Armstrong... rest in peace and tranquillity... Died
August 2012)

Silence...

Not a single soul within a radius of five miles...
Strapped rudely atop of the most powerful machine ever
[devised by humanity,
At the centre of the silent circle...
My two colleagues and I...
The seconds tick by... in reverse they count...downward.

Down there, beneath our horizontal backs,
The monster begins to stir.
Strange and distant rumbles, vibrations... emanations...
Three hundred and sixty feet below...

The sky is powder blue through the tiny triangular portal in
[front of me.
Capcom... calm and confident.
Systems check.

"All systems are go..."
Roger that...

(Ten... nine... eight... seven...)

Guidance is internal...
The pumps kick in.
Vibration, noise, the beginning of something...

(... six... five... four... three...)

Ignition.
The control panels shake so much that I cannot make them
                                                      [out,
Switches buttons and lights blur together as the monster
                                                [awakens below.
I concentrate on the powder blue portal...

(... two... one...)

Lift off.

Five titanic F-1 engines spit thunder and fire in perfect unison,
As they delicately gimbal and balance the seventeen storey
                                          [cryogenic guts of the beast.
For a moment, the monster hangs suspended, a slender
                                                [vertical pencil,
Impossibly balanced on five colossal columns of fire.
The cacophony of the engines carries for miles around the
Florida Everglades,
Causing reverberations around the world.

Numbers are rolling by, clocks are counting, dials begin to
                                                      [register.
I feel the gentle gimbaling of those mighty, roaring engines,
                                          [through the seat of my pants.
The altimeter begins to count, upward... two hundred and
forty thousand miles to go.
It's hard to discern if we are actually moving,
It doesn't feel as if we've left the ground...

"You have cleared the tower..."
Roger that.

T-plus two minutes and counting.
I'm glad I'm strapped in...
The monster relentlessly throttles its engines, mercilessly
                    [draining away its life blood.
The belly of the beast now almost empty after only two or
                    [three minutes.
I'm six times heavier as we hurtle toward the void...

Main engines shut down... staging... from five G's to
                    [free-fall...
The empty guts are discarded, the F-1 engines go with it,
Never to be used again... more checks... momentary
                    [weightlessness.
Free-falling...

IGNITION!

Heavy again!
Things to do, no time to think, more G's, more acceleration...
                    [a longer burn at this second stage.
The portal turns to a deep naval blue... and then to black...
                    [four minutes pass...
Engine shut down, another empty belly for the Pacific...
                    [weightlessness again!
Free falling... to the Moon.

As we match our rate of descent at seventeen and a half
                    [thousand miles per hour...
Into Low Earth Orbit...
Time to unite with our tiny spidery lander...
Separation from the spiders protective cocoon...
We orientate for docking, a gentle kiss in the black vacuum...

As the good Earth passes by below.
It's hard not to look at it.
Concentrate on the job in hand!
Everywhere, the infinite abyss, impenetrable blackness...
Two orbits and we're done... good job.

"You are go for Trans-Lunar Injection..."
Roger that.

(... three... two... one...)

A new, single engine ignites, we have full control.
Gravity again... nought to three G's...
I feel like throwing up.
We are on our way to the Moon.

For the first time, the Earth comes into the window.
At last we see the whole planet as a single entity.
A breathtakingly blue, green, brown and white ball.
The Sun glints off the Pacific Ocean, it dazzles and shines,
In contrast to the black eternal night of the vacuum in which
                                                    [it drifts.
Fragile.
Alone.
A giant, self regulating, four billion year old space-ship
                              [carrying every living thing,
Everything we know, through a mysterious and unknown
                                                    [universe.
All Humanity is there, through that tiny portal window.
As one.

As the radius of the Earth diminishes, so the Moon's increases.
Past the Lagrange points and the Moon begins to tug at our
                                                    [tiny craft.

We are going "down-hill" now, free wheeling faster to our
[target.
After two Earthly days, the Moon slowly begins to fill the
[window.
As the good Earth shimmers behind us, vibrant with colour...
[life...
So the Moon looms... stark, grey and lifeless.
Dead.
Sterile.
Its surface battered and scarred over ravages of immeasurable
[spans of time,
And almost continual bombardment..
A billion year onslaught...
With no atmosphere to erase the scars of impacts,
Preserved in the zero pressure vacuum for eons to come.
History is written there...
Soon to be made...

"You are go for Lunar Orbit..."
Roger that...

(... four... three... two... one...)

Our solitary engine re-ignites... Gravity, more simulated
accelerated Gravity,
This time the engine turned toward the Moon, to park our
[minute life-boat into a sixty mile Orbit.
Into the Dark side, ten times faster than a bullet.
As we pass into the Moons shadow...
Capcom wishes us luck and all communications die until
[we re-emerge on the other side.
Suddenly, we are the loneliest men in the Universe, Isaac
Newton in the driving seat.
And everywhere, stars!

All at once, the heavens display their ethereal splendours
                                       [for our eyes only.
The face of the moon starless and black as pitch.
And before us, the glory of God.

The Lander is built for two.
We will re-unite with our colleague, if all goes well,
In ten to twelve hours from now.
So many things could go wrong,
So we don't think about it.
We do what needs to be done.
We have two minutes worth of thrust in the tank to get us
                                       [safely to the surface.
The vacuum seems to suck at our fragile little craft.
The departure engine beneath us is a one shot pony,
If it doesn't light up we will not be leaving the Moon...
If something goes wrong, we can use it to abort the mission...
                                       [if it lights.
So many unknowns...
Three billion pairs of eyes...watch.

The altimeter fails.
Alarms go off.
Warning lights.
A computer glitch...too much information!
Reset the computer.

"You are go for landing..."
Roger that...

The descent engine lights up.
We go in feet first, standing.
We have a minutes worth of fuel to get us down...

Silence.

Levelling out now... coasting... surface features flying by.
Craters, boulders, rock-fields pass below in magisterial
[silence.
Ahead, a boulder field... no where safe to land... decision...
[made.
I imagine two bone-white skeletons preserved in space-suits
[forever in the wreckage,
On the sea of Tranquillity.
Twenty seconds of thrust remain...
Light it up... get over the boulder-field...
There!!

Ten seconds in the tank, twenty five feet from the surface...
In too fast!
More throttle...
Seven seconds in the tank... fifteen feet... surface lights...
[kicking up dust... Moon-dust..
More throttle..
Four seconds in the tank... a foot remains between the
[spider-legs and the surface of another world...
Descent engine shut down...
We fall the last six inches...

"Tranquillity base here... the Eagle has landed..."
"That's one small step..."

FUTURE IMPERFECT

All the stuff you think about.
All the stuff that fills your head.
All the stuff you ever learned.
Everything you've ever read.

Every image you have seen.
Every word you ever heard.
Every place that you have been.
Every moment you have spurned.

All the people you have known.
All the sorrow you have felt.
Opportunities you have blown.
All the bad cards you've been dealt.

All the feelings that you hide.
Thoughts left unexpressed.
All the pointless things you chide.
All the times you've been depressed.

Every bus that you have missed.
Deadlines that pass you bye.
All the women you have kissed.
All the times you have denied.

Aspirations turn to dreams.
Months turn into years.
Sparkles turn to gleams.
Ambition turns to fear.

Admiration turns to envy.
Fidelity to contempt.
Desire turns to avarice.
Comfort turns to discontent.

Years turn into months.
Months turn into days.
Days turn into seconds.
That we fritter all away.

All the time that you have lost.
Feeling sorry for your soul.
In terms of human cost.
The sum is smaller than the whole.

All the things that you have bitched.
All the stuff that you pooh-pooh.
Everyone that you have stitched.
Will all come back to you.

What did you create?
What else did you do?
Who did you inspire?
And what inspired you?

What do you think of?
At any moment of the day?
What gives you the impetus,
To carry on this way?

What do you really do,
With the moments that you crave?
Worry for your image.
Gossip to the grave.

The future looked so rosy.
Now there's no time to reflect.
Squandered by your vanity.
And future imperfect.

THE GOOD DEED

Trapped inside this shrivelled shell.
Through cataracts and misty veils.
My heart yet still, beats in this husk
Of wrinkled skin and bone.

Memory is my solace now.
Will I be re-born again somehow?
Regard this shrunken carcass,
Soon bereft of life, yet still,
I live and breath... I exist.
In this tiny mortal space, I persist...
Once a human being...

This dead meat that once was me.
Kept alive by sleek machinery.
A bed, a tomb, a sterile cell.
Through the window I can see the sky.

Nurses feed me liquid food.
Supplied to me through plastic tubes.
They talk to me in platitudes,
And there's nothing I can do.
I cannot move.
I want to shout...
Turn me off!
I've had enough!

But the relic on the bed.
Has said everything that could be said.
Through the window, I can see the stars,
And to them I long to return.

I tell them,
Look at the stars!
The countless stars!
The forges of life.
I yearn to go...
But the nurses just carry on filing their nails,
Or jotting down details,
From the sleek machines.

They wait for me to die.
Restrained and chained unto this rock,
Dignity I once had,
Now transformed into a hospital smock.
My adolescent mind still very much alive.
I plead for them to let me go.
For ever.

THE END OF EVERYTHING

Cars run out of petrol.
Pens run out of ink.
And soon the Earth's resources.
Will run out one day I think.

The Sun will use its hydrogen.
Trains run out of steam.
Fly-wheels lose momentum.
Minds run out of dreams.

Earth's slow and gradual spin,
Is also slowing down.
Its axial rotation.
One day will cease to go around.

My computer's out of memory.
Its circuits are corrupt.
The chips are down and wearing out.
It is set to self-destruct.

The friction is increasing,
With no oil to lubricate.
The telephones are busy,
But we don't communicate.

The seas are getting warmer,
Their levels on the rise.
Carbon dioxide readings,
Already compromised.

Soon we'll have no ice-caps,
At either of the poles.
Soon we won't need money,
Maybe soon, we'll lose control.

We build dreams from bits of paper,
Our hearts desires in coins of gold.
Embrace this culture based on envy,
And let the money damn our souls.

On this planet full of water,
Not much is fit to drink.
The destitute get poorer,
The rich don't stop to think.

The Sun will spend its gaseous fuel,
Four thousand billion years from now,
The Earth will be but as a cinder,
As the Universe winds down.
Our home spins in the vacuum,
So white and blue and green.
The Earth and its resources,
Is no perpetual machine.

I will fast run out of paper,
And the ink will soon be gone.
Are we running out of life?
At this rate it won't take long.

If we reach the end of everything,
The end of time, of life, of night.
Could the Universe begin again?
From the void, let there be light...

DEOXYRIBONUCLEIC ACID

There are instructions in my acids.
I could have been born straight or gay.
I may go bald as I get old.
So says my D.N.A.

I might have had a hairy back.
Or a tiny little knob.
Whatever I developed.
The D.N.A was on the job.

But surely a transvestite.
Cannot blame his genes.
For his urge to put on stockings.
And to straighten up the seams?

The instructions to construct me.
Lie in my every single cell.
In a minute double helix.
That can also clone itself!

Is this the core of evolution?
The reason we exist?
This tiny chain of molecules.
That around each-other twist?

I find it rather scary.
That I AM my D.N.A.
I could be replicated.
In many different ways.

Is who I am the outcome,
Of mutated chromosomes?
A minor variation,
Of my particular genome?

Am I basically the product,
Of self replicating genes?
A pre-programmed automaton,
A living flesh and bone machine?

The diversity of life,
Every unique living thing.
Has originated from,
This microscopic primal string.

Unsuccessful versions die.
They must adapt or face extinction.
Each environment must strive,
To produce genes of high distinction.

Changes in each habitat.
Produce in them varied creatures.
Modified and adapted.
With (r)evolutionary features.

What will happen to our genes,
As we change the world to suit our needs?
Surely we will stop evolving,
And our D.N.A will go to seed?

NO DRUGS TONIGHT

There'll be no drugs tonight.
None of that shite.
No substance or chemical treat.
No E's or whizz,
Just a brew and a cig,
And something substantial to eat.

There'll be no fornication,
No adulteration,
No sexually transmitted disease.
No itching of crabs,
No nasty black scabs,
Just a nice cup of tea if you please.

I won't piss my pants,
I will lay off the rants,
To be pleasant and calm will be nice.
I won't do any pills,
I'll just sit down and chill,
And take a vacation from vice.

I'm gonna keep off the grass,
Keep my hands to the mast,
Give my organs and senses a rest.
No more alcohol haze,
Paralytic and crazed,
No more mood swings and feeling depressed.

As for crack and cocaine,
I would rather abstain,
They never did too much for me.
Though the acid and shrooms,
Sent me off to the moon,
It isn't where I want to be.

Total rest for my nerves,
Nothing less I deserve,
My appointment with reality.
Give my brain cells a chance,
More time-out from my rants,
A rain-check from insanity.

Will it do any good,
This respite from the drugs?
Well, a change is as good as a rest.
Will my conformity,
Get the better of me?
And society be so impressed!(?)

We'll see how it goes,
With these substances froze,
In reality's ultimate trip.
My exploits extolled,
The trips put on hold,
So goodnight, time for bed, toodle pip.

THE ILLUSION OF TIME

Our hearts beat the steady tick,
Of the measure of our lives.
Our involuntary yardsticks,
A steady rhythm set into time.

In hours, minutes, seconds days and weeks,
We chart a course.
But briefly do our candles burn,
To fill us with remorse.

Locked in three dimensions,
Sojourning through the Milky-way.
Two hundred thousand years,
Equal of one Galactic Day.

From months to years to centuries,
And new millennia.
Epochs, aeons, eternity,
Since the Universe began.

In the beginning, was The Nothing,
If such an abstract thought could "be".
As a thought consists of "something",
Requiring consciousness, to be perceived.

The evidence before us,
Overwhelms our feeble minds.
We have long been locked away,
In this imaginary time.

Our Earthly time is measured,
Divided into equal parts,
At reassuring intervals,
As in the beatings of our hearts.

On the surface of our planet,
Every timepiece will agree,
As we hurtle around our little star,
At much the same velocities.

As our Sun ploughs through its orbit,
Around the lonely Milky-way,
If we sum up these velocities,
The data has a lot to say.

As velocity increases,
So our masses increase too,
And time begins to stretch,
With no adverse effect on you!

Your clock runs ever slower,
If ever you increase your speed,
Yet to you the seconds tick away,
Just as before, and all agree!

A Universe in motion,
Expanding into what?
Constant acceleration,
Will time eventually stop?

Time is everything and nothing,
A consequence of speed and mass.
Its existence has no substance,
Yet we still observe it pass.

The speed limit of the Cosmos,
These electromagnetic waves,
The particles we are made of,
In this same way behave.

As we approach the Speed of Light,
And seconds pass as years,
Shall we cross into that realm,
And realise our fears?

Shall we then be immortal?
As the atoms in our bones?
Shall our masses then be infinite?
Will we ever really know?

In the sub-atomic realm,
As we de-accelerate,
Will our masses then decrease?
And will Time accelerate?

As our mass and speed diminish,
Will rates of time increase until,
Time is passing at the Speed of Light,
Would its effect then thus be nil?

Time has no direction,
No velocity or mass,
No ending no beginning,
No future and no past.

We're trapped within the warp and weft,
The fabric of infinity,
Mass and speed and energy.
The truly holy trinity.

SHUT THE FUCK UP

In my head, "things" happen all at once.
As one thought occurs, several others spring to mind.
Boing bonging into one another, they tend to produce even
                                        [springier notions.
My insights can be fashionable or fissionable.
I just have to have the right inkling to begin with.
The ideal idea will initiate a chain reaction.
I will then vanish into the quantum foam in the time it takes
                                        [to say, Max Plank.
In ten dimensions will I roam, a mere wisp of energy.
Neither created nor destroyed.
To wallow in my "is"-ness.

I am NOT in this book.
I'm in the ink.
I am the science brought to bear in the construction of this
                                        [pen.
I am the gravity that it utilises to ensure an even flow of ink.
I use a million instructions, issue countless commands.
That I may guide the plastic barrel with pin-point accuracy.
I do all this and keep on thinking.
Without thinking.

I am NOT doing this.
I am cleaning the house, playing the guitar AND reading a
                                        [book.

I am having abstract conversations with my-selves.
But I am NOT doing this.
The pen is doing it for me.
I have far too many other things to do other than write words
[into a book.
What is the point of writing words in a book that no one
[reads?
The pages remain empty until SOMEONE opens the book.
These words do not exist.
Like my thoughts.

THE COST OF LIVING

I would electrocute the gas-man.
Plug him right into the mains.
I'd throw the switch with relish.
And fry his greedy brains.
I can't afford the electricity,
That I need to do the deed.
They have come to cut off my supply,
As the meter I can't feed.

I can't afford my gas bill,
So my Winter will be cold.
I can't afford the mortgage,
The payments are on hold.
They send me nasty letters,
Automatically by post.
And in the FT index,
Of their profits they do boast.

I hate my gas suppliers,
They are evil to the core.
They hike the prices up in Winter,
When Summer comes they drop once more.
My electricity supply,
Very soon will be cut short.
My energy demands,
Will very soon reduce to nought.

I will build a barricade,
Behind my windows and my doors.
I will squat in my own house,
And not pay my mortgage any more.
When they come to turn my gas off,
They will not be getting in.
Neither will the Lecky men,
Their fucking hooks they all can sling.

They will have to dig the road up,
To turn off my supply.
Before I pay their exploitive bills,
I will very surely die.
Maggie shut the coal mines,
As they weren't making any cash.
At one fell swoop she shut them all,
And the unions were trashed.

Now I haven't got a fire,
In my fire place.
With no supply of coal,
The central heating took its place.
Now I can't afford the gas,
That comes in through the pipes.
And I can't afford the lecky,
For the spark with which it lights.

I can't afford the roof,
That protects my weary head.
I can't afford the premiums,
For insurance when I'm dead.
I can't afford the petrol,
So I can't afford to drive.
I can't afford the cost of living,
I can't afford to be alive.

GREG'S LIVER

The story of Greg's Liver, is a cautionary tale.
Of an organ in rebellion, because of drinking too much ale.
Now Greg's an entertainer, and music is his trade.
Licensed bars and pubs and clubs, is where he earns his pay.
At every gig and venue, free never-ending beer.
Greg's Liver did the business, without complaint each year.
It processed every pint, that came in through Greg's blood.
It took out all the shite, and all was well and good.

Greg's Liver did the business, though it was sometimes
[over-stretched.
And Greg took it for granted, it never had must time to rest.
The years went rolling by, more gigs came rolling in.
Beer always cheap or free, ever more to indulge in.
But Greg's Liver did the job, above and beyond the call.
As the booze came flooding in, it never ceased and
[processed all!
The years turned into decades, flat out Greg's Liver worked.
And its chemical reactions, ne'er failed and ne'er shirked.

The indulgence and abuse, gave Greg's Liver no respite.
It still carried on the process, of removing all the shite.
It got old before its time, and was noble in the fight.
It was tough as leather boots, on its long and lonely plight.
Greg bloated up and fattened, his paunch grew very round.

His Liver was forgotten, as someone bought another round.
But it soon became apparent, that Greg would have to act.
He would have to rest his liver, and lose the excess fat.

Doctors orders, no more drinking, and no more spicy rat.
A different way of thinking, would take good care of that.
Greg's Liver wasn't ready, and it came as quite a shock.
When the alcohol consumption, suddenly just stopped!
Greg's poor and tired Liver, was less than well prepared.
And so began the process, of its painful self repair.
It took out all the poison, that had accumulated there.
Nine litres it expelled, with not much room the spare.

Greg could have well exploded, but the doctors drained it out.
And saved it all in baggies, it was such a large amount!
Now Greg's Liver isn't happy, and it lives on tenterhooks.
In case a pint of beer, works its way into Greg's guts.
It is a mighty organ, and it has put up with much.
Its endurance is deserving, an entry in the record books.

So respect to Gregors Liver, we salute with great aplomb.
And many more years service, are certain yet to come.
And if it makes you shiver, this cautionary tale.
Just think about Greg's Liver, and slow down on the ale.

AT NIGHT

It's mostly at night.
That I write.
In spite of the absence of light.
This may seem to you, impolite.
Indeed, anti-social or contrite.
That I hide myself away during the day.
And come out mostly, at night..

To me the nights are bright.
I take great delight in the still of the air.
And embrace the cool, crystal twilight.
My feather-light thoughts ignite into tonight..

Last night, my pen was alight.
Alive with ammonites and trilobites.
Stalagmites and stalactites.
Meteorites and satellites.
And try as I might, I couldn't quite,
Get the rhymes right..

For me, there is no respite.
Despite my dead slumber of the day.
In the day, I lack bite.
No flights of fancy with which to excite.
No revelations in which to delight.
No insight.
No second sight.

But it's alright, being a parasite of the night.
For me, it's somehow right.
Almost a ritual, a rite.
I feed like the bed-mites and vampires.
On blood and fright.

Our existences are finite and brief.
Like the graphite in a 2-B pencil.
The highlights are often trite, and banal.
Maybe I talk shite.
Then for that you may smite me now,
With all your might.
But however sleight my hand may be.
And no matter what blights me.
My fight will be, forever nocturnal..

SID THE SPID

The first time I saw Sid,
I almost shit myself.
He shot out from under the telly,
And was in the very best of health.
He stood there on the carpet,
As brazen as you please.
He could keep pace with a mouse,
On him there were no fleas.

At first, it was unnerving,
When he suddenly appeared.
This arachnid was deserving,
To be respected and revered.
Although sometimes unexpected,
He could give you such a fright.
He was healthy and well fed,
Beneath the sofa in the night.

I nearly stood on him one morning,
When he ran across my toes.
He sprinted at me without warning,
From the skirting board below.
He was a rather rapid octaped,
On those eight long slender legs,
Four shiny jack-tar eyes,
Looking behind him as he sped.

Sometimes he'd hang there from the ceiling,
Motionless for hours on end.
Oft-times I'd get the feeling,
That he was watching me again.
He admittedly was creepy,
And worryingly fast.
I put his picture up on Face Book,
But his fame was not to last.

Him being such a lively fellow,
He could turn up anywhere!
He sometimes liked the bathroom,
And would scurry into there.
One day I filled the bath,
With steaming water left to cool.
And Sid was on the ceiling,
Above that boiling pool.

Well, he must have lost his footing,
And fell into that moil.
He was drowned in that deep water,
And simultaneously boiled.
Now he's gone to spider heaven,
Up the long and silken thread.
Where bathrooms have no water,
They're full of flies instead.

THE STRANGE NON–EXISTENCE OF MUSIC

Think of a tune in your head.
Close your eyes and THINK of the music.
Can you hear it?
Of course you can... but of course, you can't ACTUALLY
                    ["hear it, for it is not real.
You can IMAGINE that you can hear it, but you only really
                    ["hear" it, in your head.
No one else can "hear" it, but you.
You are creating it yourself as you go.

Our ears have evolved to perceive sound.
They pick up vibrations in the thick atmosphere we call air.
Our timpanic ear-drums vibrate in sympathy with
                    [compression waves generated elsewhere.
The compression data is relayed to our brains.
Our brains collate and assemble the data into the sounds we
                    ["hear".

Once a sound is created and then perceived, it almost
                    [instantly vanishes.
Absorbed into the air and surroundings, or reflected in a
                    [myriad differing ways,
Each echo weaker than the last, then milliseconds later is
                    [gone, forever.

As one compression wave dies it replaced with the next,
And the next,
And the next... to produce "continuous" sound.
The linear nature of sound thus ensures its non-existence.
After listening to your favourite CD, where has the music
[gone that was produced at the loudspeaker?
It still resides and plays in your head but the actual "sound"
[has all but disappeared.
Into the ether?

The essence of sound is purely mathematical and abstract.
The duration, pitch and timing of each note obeying simple
[mathematical rules.
Yet such a wealth of emotion!
The rules are simple.
Divide a whole-note event into half, then quarters, then
[sixteenths, thirty secondths etc..
Do the same with the pitch, take a note and divide its
[frequency by two, four, eight etc..
Put them together and create, a symphony.

Consider your CD player.
Put it on and press play.
A chain of wondrous events are set in motion at the speed
[of light.
A microscopic spiral of nano-sized pits etched in to the
[shiny surface of your disc begin, to spin.
Illuminated from above by a narrow laser light at right
[angles to the surface.
A sensor picks up the reflections from the surface as tiny
[pulses of light.
Each pulse generates a small electrical signal.
A signal or a pulse, is an "on".
The absence of a pulse or signal is an "off".
The "off's" are the pits diffusing the light.

A pulse can be a one (1), and the absence of a pulse, a
[nought (0).
Binary code.
A continuous queue of "off's" and "ons", an enormous line
[of noughts and ones.
Bits and bytes of information, read from the surface of your
[shiny CD.
Music that isn't there, does not exist,it is merely a description
[of the music, NOT the music itself.

The bits and bytes spell out the voltages required to produce
[movement in a magnet surrounded by copper wire.
The varying voltage changes the electrical field in which
[the magnet moves, according to the instructions etched in
to the shiny surface of your CD.
A paper cone attached to the moving coil vibrates the air in
[front of it to produce our old friends,
Compression waves.
Producing... sound, as described above.
The compression waves arrive at your ear after travelling
[across the room at over seven hundred mph,
Losing energy as they go.
As they strike your eardrum, the vibrating timpanic
[membranes movements are amplified by tiny little bones
that are attached to biological wires called nerves.
The movement is reconverted back in to electrochemical
[pulses which are relayed via your inner ear to your brain.
And wonder of wonders, the music is made real!
Instantly replaced with compression waves of more and
[more data from the vibrating air.
Continuous "packets", quanta of data.
Your eardrum now a speaker in reverse...a microphone, two
[of them...stereo!

Think of a tune in your head, any tune.
Does it really exist?

TOODLE PIP

I'll say goodbye and toodle-pip,
Tara, farewell, so long.
I'll see ya, think I'll take a trip.
And quietly abscond.

I'll toast your health and take a sip,
It's time for me to go.
I've much enjoyed your fellowship,
It's been a jolly show.

I've shared with you a kinship,
Through times both high and low.
And I am truly thankful,
Much more than you could know.

So, bye bye and au-revoire,
I know not where to go.
Fare thee well and ta-ta,
As the wind begins to blow.

The time of my departure,
Is now very close at hand.
So I must seek new pasture,
I hope you understand.

So bon-voyage, auf-weidersein,
Adeau and fond regard.
Nothing ever stays the same,
I must turn a friendly card.

I do not wallow, mope or weep,
Nor make myself abstruse.
No sorrow in my soul I'll keep,
It won't be of much use.

My candle bright, burnt at both ends,
It smoulders at the last..
The fading glow I now befriend,
As I flicker to the past..

THE BEGINNING OF THE END

When the end came,
There was no one there to observe it.
It had been coming for a long, long time.
It had been foreseen on Earth,
Some two billion years before the Earth itself became an
                                        [airless cinder,
Orbiting a dying star.
Foreseen not by human beings, as one would expect,
No... they had long since died out a billion years previous
                                        [even to that...
Self-destructed by their greed, avarice and vanity...

The new dominant species developed their culture into a
                                        [benevolent civilisation,
And reached outward, to the stars.
They knew that their Suns energy supply was finite,
As did their long forgotten ancestors, the Human Race.
They knew that eventually, they would have to leave their
                                        [cradle in the stars,
To find new worlds, with new suns.
No matter... there were four hundred billion of them to
                                        [choose from...
There was plenty of time.

The descendants of man, for another billion years or so,
Spread out into their home galaxy, the Milky Way.
They found plenty of planets, thousands in fact in nearby
[systems,
That were suitable for sustaining life...
And so they settled,
On planets that had not the time to evolve intelligent life
[forms of their own.
These planets, they adapted to their own needs,
Transforming them into paradises in their ceaseless quest
[and thirst for knowledge.

The descendants of man discovered other benign civilisations
[along the way.
They joined forces,
In their common quest for knowledge that all benign
[civilisations crave.
They co-existed peacefully in the Milky Way galaxy for
[another five billion years...
They became wise.
Their ultimate goal to quench their never ending appetite
[for knowledge...
The comprehension and understanding of ALL things
[became their prime directive.
They eradicated hunger, envy, war, money, wealth, religion,
In their incessant unceasing craving for knowledge...
To understand, to perceive...to be.

For billions of years, they lived this way.
They colonised every habitable planet in orbit about every
[suitable star system,
Throughout the entire Milky Way system of a hundred
[billion suns.
The galaxy teemed with the life of a thousand benevolent
[civilisations.

Their eyes looked outward still,
To the billions of other galaxies receding rapidly away from
[them,
Within the void, ever faster and faster...

Over vast Ages and countless Aeons,
The uncountable populations of the Milky Way galaxy
[endured in peace,
Until the first and second generation stars began the slow,
Yet inevitable yield to Entropy, and so they began to die.
Either by slow asphyxiation,
Choking and spluttering on the last of their scant fuel reserves,
Or to their unavoidable heat-deaths.
Or.
In extravagant outbursts of super-novae explosions,
Releasing their colossal energy stores in one last, violent
[and silent,
Terminal flash of light.
The stars of the Milky way began to dim...
The black holes did the rest...

The last survivors of the descendants of the Human Beings,
Had long since observed the Earth, and its Sun,
Fade away over the billenia that followed.
They themselves agonisingly watching each star in turn,
Diminishing and fading, succumbing to their inevitable
[demises.
They watched helplessly as all the other galaxies in the
[universe,
Receded away and eventually, disappeared over the black
[horizon.
Slowly, over the vast trillennia that ensued, they realised
[that soon,
They would be utterly alone, the distances between them
[almost infinite.

When the end came, there was no living thing to observe it.
All living things in the universe being long since dead,
Along with their energy depleted stars...
All thermonuclear reactions in the universe ceased.
All distances became infinite.
The Universe was plunged into eternal darkness...

For trillions of years more, the cold, pitch-tar black universe
                          [continued to expand.
The invisible expansion, accelerating into the eternal
                          [emptiness of the infinite...

When the end did come, there was no one there to observe it.

The end came quite suddenly,
And unexpectedly,
With a big bang...

When the beginning started...
There was no one there to observe it...

'ETC'S ETC

I'm sure it must be my turn next.

I've made the calls and sent the texts.

I apologise and genuflect.

I didn't mean to disrespect.

I let you down now you're upset.

I forgotten you and now your vexed.

But looking back in circumspect.

My decisions I do not regret.

My conscience clear but imperfect.

As I sit here and now reflect.

And question my own intellect.

I don't know what I might expect.

So please feel free to interject.

You can call me on my phone direct.

Just dial the number and connect.

Into the mouthpiece then inflect.

This difference there to disinfect.

If my apologies you do reject.

Our paths will cease to intersect.

ON AWAKENING

I have awoken again, tired, confused and breathless.
Tearing the feathers from the roof of my mouth
And wiping the tears from my eyes,
Trying to focus on this page.
Exhilarated and depressed.
Covered in sweat.
Yet still in my dream, vivid and real.
Like a Spielberg movie, alive and aware.

And my loves, my children where there,
Like we used to be,
When we were family.
On a roller-coaster, happy and free once again.
I woke up alone in my bed,
Confused and and frightened.
How I miss them.
Sometimes I feel helplessly alone.

But, though I don't see them, and the dream recedes,
I remember their faces.
Oh how I miss them now,
Foolish and alone in this bed.
I cry at the unusual dream.
I remember, I really do.

I wasn't very good really.
Not much of a son, or a dad, or husband.
Not even a man.
Was I so selfish, so unattainable, so remote?
So now it hurts.
Now, after everything...
Now it hurts.
It hurts in my dreams and my head.
Makes me feel numb and strange.
More alone.
I feel ill.
Poorly in my mind, dark and secluded.
No one knows me, not even me.

If I'm to die a slow death.
Please let me go quietly nuts on my own.
My life is unreality.
I have never known how to love.
I still don't know, even now.
I feel so very isolated.
Oh how I miss my children.
So much!

At times, the loneliness is unbearable.
I have no one.
I have made-up my own life.
Sometimes it feels like a fiction,
And I wonder if any of those things I remember, really
happened.
Everywhere I look there are questions.
But no answers.
Great chunks of nothingness.
The Black...The Void.
Huge tracts of emptiness where memories should reside.
Why can't I remember?
Why the fuck can't I recall?

This is my loneliest day, my very worst.
I don't know who I am, or if I will ever find out.
What did I do?
What must I have done to be deserted so?
I really don't know.
The alien inside me has been with me for so long...
I have grown accustomed to it.

I'm so very confused today.
Please someone tell me.
Let me know who I am.
Where I came from.
Who made me.

If I could use the off-switch,
I would right now.
I have had my fill of myself, I really have.
I feel such a cunt.

I let everyone down.
What was I supposed to do?
I just didn't know.
So I made it up,
Made myself an outer-skin,
To camouflage the non-entity underneath.

I did nothing with myself, with my mind.
I went with the flow.
Though my mind was agile and quick.
I chose the easy way, and hid.

I was so used to myself, my known quantities,
And my love of the black, star-spangled night.
I never thought I would need anyone,
Because I wasn't like them.

I looked the same,
But I wasn't.
And still I look the same, and am not.

Calming now, tears drying up.
But yet still, I see the after-images of my dream,
Vivid and bright.
I love my children so,
The only love I have ever known.
It's so hard for me to tell them.
To say it.
Why can I only tell these blank white pages how I feel?
Perhaps the contrast of the nightmares,
Has enhanced the joy of it.
Have I been to sleep?
I couldn't say, but I'm so tired.
I could sleep.

I feel my life is nearly done.
Like everyone does I suppose.
I've let it go and cannot ignore... The Void.
It draws me, sucks at me, yearns for me to explore it.
I peer into its bottomless depths,
Where flickering lights come and go in the darkness.
Always just out of reach,
On the edge of the night.

What does it matter?
I WILL die,
That will be that.
Always, I felt guilt just by existing, by being alive.
I don't think I was ever meant to be.
It is as if I was an unfortunate accident,
Or a mistake.

I keep thinking of the past... but it is void.
How could I have missed it?
How could I have over-looked the past?
How can it be so black and empty?

I wasn't much of a son, or a father, brother, husband, grandson.
I made it up.
I made it all up.
I filled in the empty spaces the best I could.
I wish it wasn't me.
I never wanted, to be.
Perhaps I have been insane all along.

SILLY INTERLUDE

Please forgive me for I must intrude,
With this poetic interlude.
Though prose is nice and very fine.
And I've understood it line by line.
So I propose some silliness.
A verse dressed up in frilly-ness.
Some general silly-billy-ness.
This impromptu pantomime.

Your head is always in a book.
A recipe of words to cook.
A sentence or a paragraph.
That hopefully will coax a laugh.
So I demand some fun and mirth,
To chuckles, chortles, please give birth!
Let's see how much a laugh is worth.
Let us revel in acting daft.

A good dose of frivolity,
Would add much too the jollity.
To produce a laugh of quality,
Is the highest of ideals.
If I make you smile with this small farce.
On the town-hall steps, I will show my arse.
Into a microphone will I then fart.
Do you think this would appeal?

If you go back to that boring prose.
I will stamp my feet and tweak your nose.
I will save up all the sticky crows.
And apply them to my balls.
And from the ceiling I will hang.
Till my hair falls out or my nuts go bang.
And after the Fat Lady's sang.
I'll conform with protocol.

Oh frivolity and lunacy are what I now desire.
Nonsensical and meaningless I think may be required.
A parody of a parody would leave me well inspired.
An answer to my question, before I have enquired.
Did the bullet leave the chamber before the gun was fired?
Did the housewife shag the milkman out of love and not
[desire?
Did the kettle tell the pot to set the frying pan on fire?
Are black-holes really worm-holes and do Eskimos perspire?

It's nice that we can intersperse,
These solemn words with silly verse.
Tongue in cheek and unrehearsed,
It is a sheer delight.
But now it's time to take my leave,
No doubt you all will be relieved,
And heave a sigh and be not peeved,
Goodbye, farewell, goodnight.

IN THE COUNTRY

Pigs go oink, dogs bark and woof,
the spotty cows go moo.
The sheep all bleat and eat green grass,
and produce a lot of pooh.

The skylarks trill as the swine eat swill,
the cats eye up the birds.
The chickens cluck at the quacks of ducks,
the bacon chops have no compare.

The bees go buzz and the humbugs hum,
and the crickets chirp and drone.
Frogs belch and croak as they catch flies,
with their long prehensile tongues.

Barn owls hoot and the mice go squeak,
as the grass snakes hiss and crawl.
The mice mooch in the mulch and grass,
oblivious to it all.

The snakes eat mice and the owls eat snakes,
it's a meal within a meal.
And the snakes lay eggs but they don't have legs,
in the grass so well concealed.

The cockerel crows at the hens below,
and the bullocks snort and stomp.
The moles now go in their dark warm holes,
to catch the worms on which they chomp.

The horses neigh and the donkeys bray,
The geese all whoop and hiss.
The jackdaws caw and the mules eeyor,
what cacophony is this!

The sparrows tweet and the baa-lambs bleat,
spiders spin their traps with ease.
The bugs and flies don't realise,
that the cows have all got fleas.

The fleas suck blood and the bovine itch,
as they swish and shake their tails.
The farmer herds them to the barn,
to fill his empty pales.

High in the thatch, the beetles scratch,
There are swallows in the eaves.
The magpies taunt the farmyard cats,
as they feed their hungry breeds.

When the Sun goes down there are different sounds,
as the Summer evening draws.
The flaps of bats and the squeals of rats,
trapped in foxes jaws.

In the twilight fields as the church-bells peel,
the cuckoos roost at dusk.
In the fading light the moths take flight,
to release their secret musk.

As the farmer sleeps, the silence creeps,
stars spangle high above.
Then nothing stirs in the warm night air,
in the countryside I love.

THE GASOMETER

It has stood there for as long I can remember.
Huge and forbidding...
Hulking over the town
Like a gargantuan Dalek...

EXTEEEEEERMINATE!!!!!

Cold, grey and dispassionate.
Scary... dangerous.

There used to be two,
But somewhere in my past,
The other one... disappeared...
Someone stole it when I wasn't looking..
Or,
Perhaps,
It ignited its own gas supply one night, and even now,
Silently orbits the Earth,
Enjoying the view..

Once, when I was... (Younger?)...
We scaled the gas-works wall,
To marvel at it... The Beast.
That day, it was the same colour as the steely grey sky..

Standing close to it, I could FEEL it...
The weight of it... its gravity sucking me in...
The IMMENSITY of it...
It made me dizzy...
I was afraid of it...

EXTEEEERMMMINAAAAATE!!!!

Every day I saw it,
But after a while,
I saw it, but failed to notice it.
And very soon, it became invisible to me...
I didn't see it then for quite a number of years...

Then one day,
(When I wasn't looking)...
It re-appeared.

It looked as though it had been away for a long time.
Where ever it had been, it hadn't aged well.
Perhaps it had been and paid a visit to its twin in low-Earth
                                                    [orbit.
It must have landed badly on its return.
There were cracks in the armour.
Signs of strain...
Swathes of reddish rust spreading like a rash over its still
                                                    [fearsome hulk...

EXXXTEEERMINAAATE!

It was to disappear again for a few years,
When my children were born...

Years later, it suddenly appeared once again as my kids
[pointed up to the sky...
WASSAT?????
The rash had spread quite alarmingly...
The steely-grey skin had began to peel away...hanging in
shreds and tatters.
Torn away by the unrelenting summer sun...
It hung in long sheets, flapping hopelessly in the breeze.

EXTERMIN-AAAATE?

In recent years, my friend, the Dalek,
Has provided accommodation for a pair of equine hunters..
The Dalek takes great delight in their aerial ballet
[performances every evening.
His guests sleep safely on their iron and steel cliff...
At night,
Tiny Pipistrelle bats wheel and dive to feed their broods, as
[it creaks and groans,
In the dark.
On its long and lonely vigil,
The aches in its joints now beginning to show...

EXTERMINATE???

Goodbye my huge tin friend,
You have been EX-TERMINATED.

MERE MORTALS

We are just a happy accident,
neither special or unique.
There is no meaning to our lives,
even though this may sound bleak.

We are in no special place,
deserve no extra privilege.
We are alive and self-aware,
all seven billion hominids.

There are no gods to protect us,
we are utterly alone.
Not the centre of the universe,
but what the universe has grown.

A consequence of evolution,
our little planet here by chance.
Our Sun a star like any other,
in the infinite expanse.

And these little bits of paper,
that we care so much about.
Are just little bits of paper
that we all could do without.

We're in paradise, in heaven,
we have everything we need.
The Earth will take good care of us,
if we don't first succumb to greed.

All the stars in heaven with us,
to numerous to sum.
All the worlds that spin about them,
like our earth about the sun.

Maybe on some other planet,
a million light-years from our earth.
There's a species that has managed,
to put their species first.

We are not so very civil,
we have created rich and poor.
We have divided up our species,
and yet still divide it more.

We can't eat these bits of paper,
when the earth will yield no more.
When the planet's been depleted,
what will we use the paper for?

We are happy little accidents,
spinning in the dark?
Drifting through the cosmos,
on our fragile little ark?

We could build a civilisation,
that could travel to the stars.
This vast store of potential,
that is uniquely ours.

We observe the universe,
and so it comes to this.
If we weren't here to see it,
would the universe exist?

A GOOD NIGHT OUT

6pm.
There are many types of people, that traipse up and down
Duke Street.
On almost any night, of almost any week.
To outward appearances, they are presentable and neat.
But appearance is deceptive (you will discover as we speak).

7pm.
From a distance in the evening, it could be almost any town.
It looks a jolly place, a place were jolly-ness abounds.
The men all neat and clean, and the girls parade around.
From one end to the other, they all walk up and down.

8pm.
It is early in the evening, as we proceed along the street.
In its jolly little taverns, you can sit and rest your feet.
There are lots of jolly shops, that sell jolly things to eat.
Some places have live music, in others, jolly disco beats.

9pm.
Harems of mini-skirted ladies, in their tottering high-heels.
With tattoos on their ankles, and their cleavages revealed.
They bat their long black eye-lashes, as they display their
[wares.
The men drink more and more, and manly conversations
[share.

10pm.
They talk of rugby as they drink, their bravados on the rise.
Across the point of no return, the lager swills behind their
[eyes.
The common sense is washed away (if there was any there
[to start).
The nice girls all along the street, begin to look like tarts.

11pm.
They wobble now in their spiky heels, the condoms in their
[bags.
The ladies toilets all form queues, as they all turn into slags.
The G & T's and Wicked's now, begin to take their tolls.
They plaster on more make-up, as their eyes begin to rove.

11:30pm.
The beer too is taking hold, time to get a few more jars.
The alcohol goes down their throats, in all the Duke street
[bars.
In the wallets of the inebriate, in little sealed-up plastic bags.
The cocaine and amphetamines, will surely set their tongues
[to wag.

11:50pm.
A skin-full of cheap ale and talk, with nose-fulls of cocaine.
They sweat, get agitated, looking for someone to blame.
They strut around like cockerels, and display their
[under-stains.
The mates join in and pat their backs, soon they all look the
[same.

Midnight.
The girls are in the toilets, discussing their prospects.
Whilst touching up the slap, adjusting tits to best effect.
For a taxi ride and alco-pop, and a compliment of fags.

They pick and choose among the boys, the ones they want
[to shag.

12:15am.
Aggression boils and builds up, fueled by testosterone.
Latent violence is quite palpable, in its dark undertone.
The beak, the whiz and alcohol, dividing up each brain.
And now its getting hard to tell, if there are any of them sane.
The women's inhibitions, like their piss goes down the pan.
They admire a bit of violence, that's what they like in a man.
Like the ladies in the front row, that surround a boxing ring.
They aggravate the situation, with their constant heckling.

12:25am.
There are harmless drunks bewildered, gone to oblivion and
beyond.
They piss themselves and fart and burp, sing tuneless little
[songs.
The toilets stink of vomit now, the pans are full of shit.
You have to hold your breath in there, or you might gag on it.

12:30am.
The Landlord's called last-orders, they buy much more than
[they can drink.
But they serve them each and everyone, lest they kick up a
[stink.
In back-entry ways and passages, the ladies (turned to
[slags).
Drop their knickers for the knee-tremblers, who are paying
[for their cabs.

1:15am.
Theirs a fight outside the kebab shop, and as they knock
[each-other senseless.
The police drive up and carry on, so the but the boot goes
[in relentless.

There are multi-coloured vomit spills, dog ends and pizza
[cartons.
A guy has had his head kicked in, just outside of Bartons.

2:05am.
The pubs have locked and barred their doors, the street is
[strangely hushed.
The cocaine fueled maniacs, into night-clubs now are crushed.
A clean breeze stirs along the street, to lift the stink and
[paper bags.
Regurgitated pizza, bad cheese burgers and kebabs.

6:15am.
The street-sweepers are on the case, soon the street is
[squeaky clean.
The blood-stains piss and vomit, discreetly removed from
[the scene.
To all intent and purpose, this may have well been abstract.
But they'll do it all again next week, you can be sure they
[will be back.

CONTACT

I seem to get more lonely, as I age,
In spite of ever more acquaintances on my Face Book page,
Snowed under with invites to events that seem irrelevant,
As indeed, is my presence.
Year on year, the birthday cards disappear,
To be replaced with digitally recalled, electronic platitudes,
Insincere obligations delivered at the speed of light,
With the impersonal touch and habitual etiquette,
That is the protocol of the binary revolution.

Numbers are everywhere,
Too many to remember.
Our lives are reduced to numbers,
The more efficiently to plunder.
To be transformed into profit
For the in-human purveyors and peddlers
Of all the worthless shit that *they* say,
We *need*.
Indeed... even my value as a person,
Has been reduced to a number.

I might as well be a hologram,
A digital representation of me,
A memory of me.
A mere silicon slice,

The previous saved version,
Amenable and nice.
A binary number stream in your (random access) memory.
The happy, smiley me.
A digital, non-existent effigy,
Flushed away with a re-boot.

I don't see a soul for days on end,
Sometimes weeks!
I can't tell where the days begin
And the nights end.
They sort of blend,
One into the other.
Appearing indistinct in the smeared-out glue of time.
The ticks become thuds in my chest,
Beating the years into seconds,
Every year increasing the distance
And reducing the temperature
Of my human relations.

I know so many people that I *don't* know!
They serve only to quantify and enhance my isolation.
Compounding my frustration with the ironic lack
Of *meaningful* communication,
Of conversation,
Of Contact.

CUPIDS ARROW

Another bladdy Valentine,
Another card; "Will you be mine?"
A bunch of flowers,
A glass of wine,
Another bladdy Valentine.

The cheapest love you'll ever find,
With verses of the cheesy kind,
A restaurant,
Some candle light,
You're sure to get your end tonight.

Another round of "I love you"s,
Echoed by "I love you too"s,
A squeeze,
A kiss,
With no virtue,
Another bladdy year with you.

Another heap of sentiment,
The hormones taking precedent,
After-shave,
Sweet perfumes,
A fumble in a darkened room.

A token of undying love,
KY jelly, rubber gloves,
Leather whips,
SS caps,
PVC with rubber straps.

Cupids arrows everywhere,
They could land almost anywhere,
In your arse,
Or open heart,
Tell her you love her, play the part.

My love for you I do define,
With this edict, very fine,
A rose,
A kiss,
A washing line,
Please be my bladdy Valentine.

DAYLIGHT ROBBERY

Most assuredly I do attest,
Do I own up and so confess,
In earnest this I do express,
With no prevarication.
Please allow, that I may make this point,
Oh patient ears will I anoint,
No nose to be put out of joint!
From this humble dissertation.

The information so disclosed,
Within the rhetoric it flows!
(Its kernel deep inside, it grows)
As a pearl locked in an oyster.
Its moral swathed as onion skins,
Its every layer paper-thin,
Profound the words that draw you in,
To my sepulchered cloister!

In poetic speech I so beseech,
A carrot just beyond your reach,
The pulpit out of of which I preach,
These phantom revelations.
A ruse to lure you to this verse,
No ethic, though yet well rehearsed,
A rhyme for time, may it be cursed,
At its dire imagination!

Forgive me, for you have been robbed,
The time of which you have been fobbed,
Oh how the prose has ducked and bobbed,
In non-communication!
However, I have spent much time,
Constructing this contentious rhyme,
If there be loss, the loss be mine!
I call it recreation!

DUST

Having been reduced to my basic constituents,
Of twenty two commonly occurring elements,
A National Insurance number,
And a post-code.
And, having deduced,
That emotion is chemically induced,
When all is said and done...

In me this has produced,
An apathetic constitution,
A frivolous attitude.
In the scrutiny and exacting circumstances
Of the distillations and the essences of this life,
I am appalled to find that,
I am nothing more,
Than a handful of dust.

ENDINGS

Though it seems as my world is crumbling around me,
Or that all my conclusions point to endings.
And that all my endings are cliff-top suicides,
Where all roads abruptly end,
And kamikaze's fly.

When all that is left to do is die,
And I'm left with nothing but an abyssal leap of faith
Into the star-struck sky,
Or to the ragged crashing rocks below...

I yet still abide.
I endure.
I'm alive.

SUMMARY 2011

DRUM-KITS: 1 electric.

GUITARS ACQUIRED: One electric.
                    One electric Bass.
                    One classical Spanish guitar.
                    repair to broken neck/electro-
                                    [acoustic.
                    (piss-head related damage).

GUITAR STRINGS: 20 sets, of which:
                    10 acoustic.

CIGGIES: 1040 standard cigarettes.
                    156 modified cigarettes.
                    ONE highly unusual cigarette.
                    6 standard roll-ups.

LIGHTERS: 26 of which:
                    26 stolen.

BEER: 416 pints
                    (averaged over the year) of cider.

TEA: 780 cups (averaged over the year).

SHITES: 104 of which:
                    70 solid

20 large.
8 sloppy.
7 liquid.

PEES: Around 5-6oo.

VOMIT: 4 of which: 1 with carrots.
1 with carrots AND sweet corn.

SNOT: Around 1.5 pints.

CROWS & BOGIES: 75, of which:
38 flick-able.
17 roll-able.
12 sticky.
8 stringy.

SHAVES: 130.

CLOSE SHAVES: EVERYDAY.

LEMON MUFFINS: 88 (ASDA) of which:
1 stolen/returned.

STOCKINGS: 18, of which:
14 laddered.

TELLY LICENCE: 0.

HAIRCUTS: 0.

LIGHT-BULBS: 30, of which:
24 wrong fitting.

PS3 GAMES: 18, of which:
18 unfinished.

FACE-BOOK INCIDENTS: 1 major.
1 minor.
4 un-friendings.

CAUSING A SCENE: 6 (I think).

REPORTED TO THE POLICE: 2, of which:
1 bullying (!).
1 theft (!!), retracted.

WANKS: 100-120.

NOSE BLEEDS: 3.

HEAD-ACHES: 35 or so.

SLEEP: 1460 hours, of which:
400 sound.
600 fitful.
300 induced.
160 REM.

BREATHS: 28,000 per day.
806,000 per month.
3,200,000 per quarter.
12,902,400 per year.

FARTS: 170, of which:
100 loud.
40 loud and smelly.
9 wet.
16 SBD.
5 public.

BOOKS: 9, of which:
8 from charity shops.
1 new, a dear do!

REDUNDANCY MONEY: £14,000, of which:
£14,000 gone.

PHOTOGRAPHS: 2,700, of which:
1,300 musicians.
850 holidays.
450 in pubs.
200 pornographic.

BITTS FELL OFF CAR: 4, of which:
0 replaced.

HOUSE-HOLD SHITE: 235 bin-bags, of which:
175 packaging.
22 horrible gungy stuff.
16 beer-cans.
27 burnt food.

VISITS TO ASDA: 170, of which: 37 complaints.
33 incidents of queue jumping.
48 instances of trolley rage.
2 incidents of verbal violence.
15 aggravated granny attacks.
15 beggars at the entrance.
3 transvestites (including me).
27 visits to the bogs.

FAST FOOD: 83, of which:
72 bacon butties.
3 McDonalds.
3 McDonalds vomits.
8 KFC/Spicy Rat.

SIGHTINGS OF JOHNNY WELLIE: 3, of which:
1 at "Game" shop.
1 at Zoo Bar.
1 in Boots.

PETS:
1, of which:
6 shredded shirts.
3 turds in bath.
11 fur-balls in various locations.
7 instances of lacerations and
[blood-letting.
Decreased spider population.
4 hoover-fulls of cat fur.
1 cat booted out back to rightful
[owner.

ACCIDENTS:
14, of which:
3 cases of chair entanglement.
4 cases of table falls.
1 collapse (vertical).
2 backward falls from chairs.
2 table slumps.
2 follow through's.

LITTLE LUXURIES

Bog-roll... sheer luxury.
Light-bulbs... what a novelty.
No shitting in the dark for me,
I'm saving electricity.

Fray Bentos... my ambrosia.
Smart Price is my cordon bleu,
SO I do my shopping there,
When there's a bit of cash to spare.

Shoe-laces... such decadence.
A hoover... what extravagance.
Pot Noodles... Oh what opulence,
Perchance to dream of pounds and pence.

A cooker with a ring that works,
Indeed for me would be a perk,
A fridge in which some food may lurk,
A boiler, minus all the quirks.

Mental health... a state of mind.
The welfare state do I rob blind?
Each passing minute seems to grind,
Each passing hour, I lapse behind.

A car... a big white elephant,
A heap of steel, irrelevant,
A pile of ashen cash misspent,
To enrich the corporate acumen.

A mortgage... what a waste of time,
For never will my house be mine.
Would that water, turn to wine!
Benevolence, show me a sign.

ROCKET SCIENCE

Rocket science.
A piece of piss.
Or was there something,
That I missed?

A rubber balloon filled with air,
A higher pressure-difference there,
As pressure moves from high to low,
Release the teat and watch it go!
The tension in the rubber balloon,
Expels the air into the room!
A reaction engine we now see,
As the balloon moves off opposingly!

Though balloons are good analogies,
Of Newtons laws of motion three.
Too quickly they lose energy,
In flight that's less than friction-free.
Stretched rubber keeps the pressure on,
So the journey isn't very long,
The rubber shrinking back to size,
Expelling air from the inside.

So, how to keep the pressure high?

How to replace the air inside?
To maintain a steady, constant thrust,
What parameters must we adjust?
The gas inside it must expand,
Constantly and on demand!
A new balloon that does not shrink,
With a nozzle at one end I think!

Now, we might be getting there!
But what are we to use for air?
Ignite a gas, and it expands,
Explosively, it makes a bang!
A chamber to contain ignition,
A nozzle to direct emission,
A fuel source for long reaction,
An exit for exhaust extraction.

Fuel, pumped from tank to chamber,
Combustion in a closed container!
A throttle to control the flow,
On the exhaust gases, up we go!
Combustion chamber gases burn,
The exit nozzle tilts and turns,
With vector and velocity,
To point us where we want to be.

Reaction engines work in space,
A vacuum is the perfect place!
Frictionless momentum gained,
When stable orbit is attained.
Mixed hydrogen and oxygen,
In a cryogenic state,
Ignited in the chamber,
To such heights will elevate!

SHAGGING SHOES

You couldn't go out wearing them that much is true.
They spend more time up in the air,
That's because they're shagging shoes.
You couldn't push a hoover round,
That simply wouldn't do.
You'd surely trip and break your neck,
And end up black and blue.

You could maybe change a light-bulb,
But it's not recommended.
You'd only end up in the dark,
If you should get up-ended.
These shoes are sex personified,
Red patent leather hues.
These shoes are made for shagging,
Let's not be misconstrued.

Boots may be made for walking,
But these are just plain rude.
They're purely made for pleasure,
These are my shagging shoes.

SNOT

As temperatures start falling.
And icy winds begin to blow.
When the price of gas goes up.
And the Winter takes a hold.
My proboscis starts producing,
Amazing quantities of crows.
And inordinate amounts,
Of bright green snot begin to flow.

I know not where it comes from.
Or how it is produced.
The reason for its presence,
I never have deduced.
Every year guarantees,
That I will manufacture lots.
A never ending stream,
Of viscous thick green snot.

It seems a shame to waste it.
Perhaps there's something I could do.
Store it up in bottles,
And sell it off as glue.
I'm sure that it's fluorescent,
And produces its own light.
I could put it in a lava-lamp,
And watch it swirl around at night.

What is this strange secretion,
That has no purpose I can see.
I produce the stuff in gallons,
To fill a thousand handkerchiefs.
I suppose there is a meaning,
An ideology.
To keep the wheels a-turning,
In the tissue industry.

SOCIAL DECLINE

They sit in little groups,
Within the steady beeps and tones,
With one eye on each-other,
And the other on their phones.
Flying through the ether,
Indecipherable microwaves,
These virtual conversations,
That now are all the rage.

Tiny knots of social intercourse,
Where nothing much is said,
Sending messages on Face Book,
Where they still remain unread.
The air vibrates with scandal,
As they tap their mobile phones,
Their holographic babble,
Reveals them to be clones.

Enslaved to their technology,
At the pressure from their peers,
Virtual images of themselves,
Are not what they appear.
Their profiles sing and dance,
Their interests so professed,
In cyberspace they rock!
On Twitter, sent by text.

Tiny islands made of people,
Sitting face to face,
The distances between them,
Increasing at a pace.
Now and then maintain eye-contact,
But as words begin exchange,
The bleeps that sound like Morse-code,
Set them to their phones again.

So the art of conversation,
Over time it so decays,
Linguistically degraded,
Discoloured, drab and grey.
The language of frivolity,
Discourteous of speech,
The dumbing of the spoken word,
By fad and self-conceit.

SOME OTHER ISLAND

On some other island
My future unfolds
In turquoise and azure
And sunsets of gold

In inky blue twilight
The moon draws the sea
Perseids streak
Through the night-sky for me

In rock-pools and hideaways
Hidden by time
The ephemeral carapace
Scented in brine

The numberless blooms
Animated to life
The fragrance of hope
So allure and entice!

Charged and inspired
By the faith you have shown
Into ambition
My pipe-dreams have grown

My eternal gratitude
Lies at your feet
On some other island
When life is complete.

SURGICAL REMOVAL

Please pass the paracetamol,
It's time I wasn't here.
I'm sick of pissing people off,
I'm sick of counting years.
I've had enough of being me,
It's time that I was gone.
This mortal coil just weighs me down,
It's plain I don't belong.

Having tried to make the jigsaw fit,
Its image I can't see.
There seems to be a piece amiss,
Another piece of me.
It appears I was a botch job,
A patched-up afterthought.
A dubious construction,
That no one could abort.

It would be easier to disappear,
Only cunts choose suicide.
It's getting harder all the time,
To find a place to hide.
I don't want to bring you down,
I just want it to end.
Despair and loneliness prevail,
On that I may depend.

The bite-marks on the bullets,
Never did amount to much,
Having used my isolation,
As a weapon and a crutch.
As a specimen, pathetic,
As a human, even less.
As a loved-one, non-existent,
An alien to tenderness.

So I'd like to pull the plug now,
Let the dirty water go.
But I cannot find the courage,
To let the people down I know.
I can't be seen to be pathetic,
Like they, I too have foolish pride.
I am stuck with this existence,
An early death for me denied.

Whey should there be derision,
So attached to suicide?
Forced to endure misery,
That social stigma so derides.
Why can't I say I've had enough,
And bid a fond farewell?
And why must you insist,
That if I do, I'll go to hell?

I've been alive for fifty years,
I've learnt a lot of things.
The ups and downs,
The lost's and founds,
The sweetness and the stings.
The virtues and the cruelties,
The bitter twists of fate.
And always have I been alone,
With this to contemplate.

So, bin the paracetamol,
I cede death by natural causes.
This waste of space will not accept,
Your platitudes and clauses.
Go fuck your social niceties,
Your scorn and smug ideals.
Go stick your lofty moral tones,
They'll never wash with me.

I've seen the light, this waste of space,
Is on to your wee game.
In this patronising shade and hue,
You're all the fucking same.
I envy you your ignorance,
Of sufferance and more.
Your misplaced moral high-ground,
Is unwelcome at my door.

I commit my social suicide,
Public socio-ectomy.
I won't deny and will not hide,
But there'll be less of me.
As I wasn't raised as human,
I have no family.
I just have my two children,
They are all that's left of me.

TABOO

There are many anti-social things, we're not supposed to do.
Body functions and processes that are still a bit taboo.
They have existed since the dawn of man, so it's nothing
[really new.
It's not polite to burp and shite or sometimes follow-through.

A silent fart is quite an art, in pleasant company.
If you can't quell that nifty smell I'm sure you would agree.
A poker-face will save disgrace, if you cast your gaze
[elsewhere.
Try to look at someone with a cold, accusing stare.

Though gentle pumps and silent trumps are simple to expel.
It's usually not so easy to ignore the pungent smell.
So many give themselves away, the odour makes them blush.
A visit to the lavatory would have cured it in a flush.

Other people celebrate and are proud their boffs are loud.
Of their ear-piercing rippers justifiably proud.
To break wind mid-conversation is a science and an art.
Waiting for the ideal moment to squeeze out the perfect fart.

There are certain situations where are parp is not desired.
At christenings and weddings a tighter sphincter is required.
A hum-dinger tends to linger as it echoes through the cloisters.
That special moment will be lost for congregation and
[rejoicers.

When someone dies it's suicide to let one go in church.
Everyone will know it's you and leave you in the lurch.
Ironically, inside the box there is an awful smell.
The bloated corpse produces lots of burps and farts as well.

A noisy bum can be such fun as all small children know.
Some take delight and can ignite their farts to watch them
[glow.
Some sound wet and some regret, their emissions have no
[pong.
Others get embarrassed as the niff is very strong.

To fart at will can be a thrill and give great satisfaction.
In tedious conversation the most engaging of distractions.
May polite society forever frown on this compulsion.
The hilarity they fail to see as they grimace in revulsion.

So never keep them bottled up, it's bad for ones digestion.
They're always better out than in for me there is no question.
So highly entertaining and amusing yet berated.
A silent arse deserves no less than to be constipated.

THE DEVIL IN THE DETAIL

An evil devil is alive,
Reviling and vile.
His greatest skill, to kill,
To defile.

He is the mob, the bomb,
The basket-case gone wrong.
He is hatred and dearth,
The thread of this earth.

He is unclear, nuclear,
Unreal and cruel.
An every-day Joe,
A punter,
A fool.

He is a grudge
With a detonator,
Bullied at school.
A psychotic killer
With a college degrees
In chemistry and philosophy.
He's addicted to TV,
Not reality.
He's respectable,
Respectful, and cool.

He's a racist, an artist,
A malignant cyst.
A fascist, a sadist,
A non-conformist.
He's a rock-star, a wannabe,
A senator, a god.
A cleaner, a bin-man,
A vagrant,
Joe Blogs.

He's alive!
Abroad and virile!
In the net-works and telephones,
In off-handed smiles.
He's in the detail deleted,
The deeds and the files.
In the modems, the cables,
The switches, the dials.
In the casing, the circuit-board,
The timer, the fuse.
In the focus and determination to use.

The madness, the method,
The fore-thought, the act.
He's the cold calculation,
After the fact.

The devil is madness,
Disguised as a bomb.
Impossibly human,
Impossibly wrong.
A product of our
Sociological norm.
From what origin?
What evolution makes bombs?

THE 'L' WORD

Your love will be the death of me
A vice around my heart.
Constricting my identity
and taking me apart.
Your "love" is suffocating me
and choking me with rules.
This game of insecurity
Played by so many fools.

Your "love" is like a mortgage
An emotive guarantee.
That I return this "love" to you
And you give it to me.
Love's a cheap commodity
So carelessly avowed.
A common little utterance
Too often said aloud.

Our loves grow from suspicions
Of our infidelities.
Our "love" succeeds in strangling
Our individualities.
Your "love" affects my actions
So bends me to your will.
And when your "love" has ended
The scars will be there still.

"Love" is like an albatross
draped about the neck.
Becalmed upon an ocean
And chained unto the deck.
No breath of air refreshing
The stale and stagnant sea.
Monsters lurk within its depths
There to wait for me.

Your "love" will kill our friendship
And teach you to mistrust.
The germs of doubt will multiply
The blood will turn to rust.
So say that you don't "love" me
And ever be my friend.
For the day you say you "love" me
Friendship will surely end.

THE LIVING DEATH

Beyond the peripherals of vision.
Where the twilight wanes to dusk.
Just beyond the reach of hearing.
At the extremities of trust.
Betwixt vanity and insanity.
Between the vacuum and the swell.
The distant hum of constant bustle.
On this slow descent to hell.

Amid the thinning air and nowhere.
Within the fog that numbs the sound.
Atop the cliff that falls forever.
Is where the Living Death is found.
Where the split-second is infinity.
And the black is incomplete.
Where salvation hangs in tatters.
And is ever out of reach.

Here is hunger never sated.
Here be desire unsatisfied.
Amongst the dark pools with no bottom.
Across the infinite divide.
The dead centre of the black hole.
Free-falling without end.
Event horizon still receding.
Around the never-ending bend.

Locked in suspended animation.
Aware of every frozen frame.
Where every image in the sequence.
Is exactly the same.
Amid the silence that is deafening.
The over-bearing emptiness.
Where there is everything and nothing.
Dwells the immortal Living Death.

UNDESIRABLE ELEMENTS

… (She was pissed as a fart that night).

She laddered her tights,
When her fag dropped (alight),
Into her inviting lap...
There was no burn to be discerned,
On that smooth expanse of thigh,
So generously displayed,
Now compelling each lecherous eye...
Yet still, she was saddened at the ladder,
(Even though she was bladdered)
On her thigh...

You may say it looked tart,
Perhaps tending toward smut,
But in part, (And in truth),
It was well known,
That she *was* a bit of a slut.
Which had the net effect,
(as one would expect)
Of attracting the attention,
(With all due respect)
Of the undesirable elements at the bar.

VALID INVALID

Am I an artist or a slob?
A poet or a leech?
Liability or asset?
Victory or defeat?

Am I enlightened or deluded?
Exulted or confused?
Entitled or excluded?
Empowered or bemused?

Preservation, demolition?
Rejection or redemption?
Pipe-dreams or premonition?
Insight or pretension?

Am I a human or a termite?
A person or a part?
A certified transvestite,
Is is trash or is it art?

Am I valid or invalid?
Redundant or in use?
Valuable or worthless?
Another lame excuse?

Have I a purpose or an import?
Have I very much to share?
Do I waste my time in idle thought?
With so very little spare?

WHAT'S LOVE GOT TO DO WITH IT?

An axe to grind,
A bone to pick,
A hair to split in two.
A fault to find,
A dog to kick,
An argument with you.

A knife to twist,
A curse to spit,
The daggers from your eyes.
An icy stare,
The frigid air,
The bullets on stand-by.

That wedded-bliss,
Should come to this,
From heaven unto hell.
Insanity,
Profanity,
How vanity impels.

Mistaken love,
A boxing glove,
A weakness in the knee.
The butterflies,
The alibis,
The bad-smell on the the breeze.

Such little things,
Now hornet-stings,
Malicious in contempt.
The venom drips,
From narrowed lips,
In cold malevolence.

The passion gone,
The years drag on,
A carbon-copied haze.
Hard to conceal,
The way we feel,
Like dragons in a cage.

A limb to hack,
A heart attack,
Incisions to be made.
Dissect the parts,
The head, the heart,
And go our separate ways.

YOU ARE HERE

Here I am,
This is me,
What you get is what you see.
No airs no graces,
This is it,
An asset or a heap of shit?
The scabs the scars,
The warts and all,
The closet skeletons and gaul.
The heart the sleeve,
The open wounds,
The mire, the swamp,
The dark lagoon.

Here I am,
For good or ill,
The tonic and the bitter pill.
The Summer breeze, the Winter chill,
The tax-rebate, the unpaid bill.
Here I be,
A metaphor,
For everything that you deplore.
A punch-bag with no heart I'm sure,
An irritation at your door.
Please excuse my hard reality.

My faults, my flaws,
My vanity.
Short-fallings,
My profanity,
My insanity,
This thing I be.

Here I am,
The best I can,
The me I try to understand.
The me that tries so hard to see,
The me I sorely want to be.
Here I go,
Another show,
Another high, another low.
The other me I'll never know,
The me I've tried to nurture so,
The me that never seems to grow.